BOOKWORMS

LET'S EXPLORE THE OCEAN!

By Nicole Horning

Cavendish Square

New York

Published in 2021 by Cavendish Square Publishing, LLC
243 5th Avenue, Suite 136, New York, NY 10016

Copyright © 2021 by Cavendish Square Publishing, LLC

First Edition

Website: cavendishsq.com

This publication represents the opinions and views of the author based on his or her personal experience, knowledge, and research. The information in this book serves as a general guide only. The author and publisher have used their best efforts in preparing this book and disclaim liability rising directly or indirectly from the use and application of this book.

All websites were available and accurate when this book was sent to press.

Library of Congress Cataloging-in-Publication Data

Names: Horning, Nicole, author.
Title: Let's explore the ocean! / Nicole Horning.
Description: First edition. | New York : Cavendish Square Publishing, 2021. | Series: Earth science explorers | Includes index.
Identifiers: LCCN 2019049087 (print) | LCCN 2019049088 (ebook) |
ISBN 9781502656278 (library binding) | ISBN 9781502656254 (paperback) |
ISBN 9781502656261 (set) | ISBN 9781502656285 (ebook)
Subjects: LCSH: Ocean–Juvenile literature. | Marine animals–Juvenile literature. |
Climatic changes–Juvenile literature.
Classification: LCC GC21.5 .H697 2021 (print) | LCC GC21.5 (ebook) | DDC 551.46–dc23
LC record available at https://lccn.loc.gov/2019049087
LC ebook record available at https://lccn.loc.gov/2019049088

Editor: Nicole Horning
Copy Editor: Nathan Heidelberger
Designer: Rachel Rising

The photographs in this book are used by permission and through the courtesy of: Cover Dmitry Polonskiy/Shutterstock.com; p. 5 Aphelleon/Shutterstock.com; p. 7 TaLyDes/Shutterstock.com; p. 9 icemanphotos/Shutterstock.com; p. 11 andrey polivanov/Shutterstock.com; p. 13 Andrey Armyagov/Shutterstock.com; p. 15 trgrowth/Shutterstock.com; p. 17 Volodymyr Goinyk/Shutterstock.com; p. 19 Chase Dekker/Shutterstock.com; p. 21 divedog/Shutterstock.com; p. 23 Hurst Photo/Shutterstock.com.

Some of the images in this book illustrate individuals who are models. The depictions do not imply actual situations or events.

CPSIA compliance information: Batch #CS20CSQ: For further information contact Cavendish Square Publishing LLC, New York, New York, at 1-877-980-4450.

Printed in the United States of America

Find us on

CONTENTS

A World of Water!

Water is very important to people, animals, and plants. Some of Earth's water is found in lakes, in rivers, or as ice. Some is under the ground. However, most of Earth's water can be found in its oceans.

5

Oceans cover more than half of Earth. The five oceans are the Atlantic Ocean, Pacific Ocean, Indian Ocean, Arctic Ocean, and Southern Ocean. They're all **connected**, but each ocean is different. Some are hotter, and some are colder.

Map of Oceans

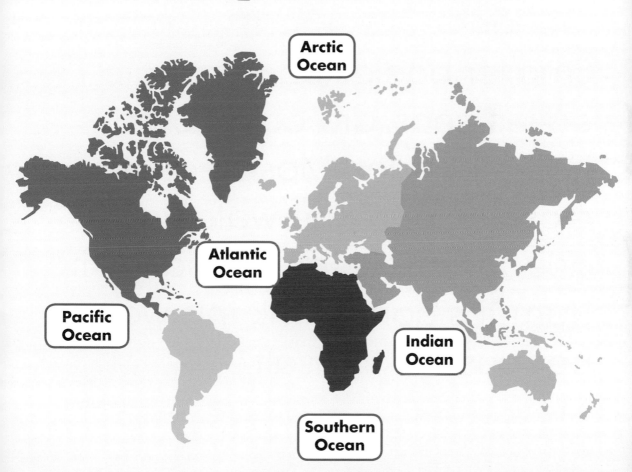

Arctic Ocean

Atlantic Ocean

Pacific Ocean

Indian Ocean

Southern Ocean

Smaller bodies of water, called seas, are connected to the oceans. Most seas are close to land. The water in oceans and seas has salt in it. Humans can't drink this water because of the salt.

Oceans and Weather

Oceans play a big part in why different places have different kinds of weather. Oceans hold on to heat to keep Earth warm. They also help move heat around the world.

11

Ocean **currents** move warm and cold water around the world. Without ocean currents, it would be too hot in some places and too cold in others. It would be harder to live on Earth.

13

Water on Earth is always moving. First, ocean water evaporates, which means it enters the air. Later, it forms clouds and falls to the ground as rain or snow. This water then flows to the ocean, and the **cycle** starts again.

The Water Cycle

clouds form

rain or snow

evaporation

water flows to oceans

Ocean Life

Millions of plants and animals live in the ocean. However, a lot of the ocean still hasn't been explored, or visited, by people. There could be many more animals and plants in the ocean that haven't been discovered yet!

The ocean is home to plants and animals of many sizes. Some are so small they can't be seen by people's eyes. The ocean also is home to the largest animal on Earth, which is the blue whale!

19

Plants that live in the ocean make oxygen, which is in the air people breathe. We need oxygen to live! More than half of the oxygen people and animals breathe comes from the ocean.

Garbage can get into the ocean and hurt the plants and animals that live there. Picking up garbage and recycling what you can are ways to help keep the ocean clean. Everyone can do their part!

WORDS TO KNOW

connected: Joined together.

currents: Parts of the ocean moving in a set way.

cycle: Something that happens over and over again.

garbage: An unwanted object that has been thrown away.

INDEX

24